First Poems

OF CHILDHOOD

Illustrated by Tasha Tudor

PLATT & MUNK, PUBLISHERS
A DIVISION OF GROSSET & DUNLAP

Monday's Child

Monday's child is fair of face,
Tuesday's child is full of grace,
Wednesday's child is full of woe,
Thursday's child has far to go,
Friday's child is loving and giving,
Saturday's child works hard for its living,
And a child that's born on the Sabbath day
Is fair and wise and good and gay.

Baby

By GEORGE MacDONALD

Where did you come from, baby dear?
Out of the everywhere into the here.

Where did you get those eyes so blue?
Out of the sky as I came through.

What makes the light in them sparkle and spin?
Some of the starry spikes left in.

Where did you find that little tear?
I found it waiting when I got here.

What makes your forehead so smooth and high?
A soft hand stroked it as I went by.

What makes your cheek like a warm white rose?
I saw something better than anyone knows.

Whence that three-cornered smile of bliss?
Three angels gave me at once a kiss.

Where did you get this pearly ear?
God spoke, and it came out to hear.

Where did you get those arms and hands?
Love made itself into hooks and bands.

Feet, whence did you come, you darling things?
From the same box as the cherubs' wings.

How did they all just come to be you?
God thought about me, and so I grew.

But how did you come to us, you dear?
God thought about you, and so I am here.

The Months

By RICHARD B. SHERIDAN

January snowy,
February flowy,
March blowy;

April showery,
May flowery,
June bowery,

July moppy,
      August croppy,
            September poppy;

October breezy,
      November wheezy,
            December freezy.

Pussy Willow

By KATE L. BROWN

Pussy Willow wakened
    From her winter nap,
For the frolic spring breeze
    On her door would tap.

"It is chilly weather
    Though the sun feels good.
I will wrap up warmly,
    Wear my furry hood."

Mistress Pussy Willow
    Opened wide her door.
Never had the sunshine
    Seemed so bright before.

Never had the brooklet
    Seemed so full of cheer:
"Good morning, Pussy Willow,
    Welcome to you, dear!"

Never guest was quainter:
    Pussy came to town
In a hood of silver gray
    And a coat of brown.

Happy little children
    Cried with laugh and shout,
"Spring is coming, coming,
    Pussy Willow's out."

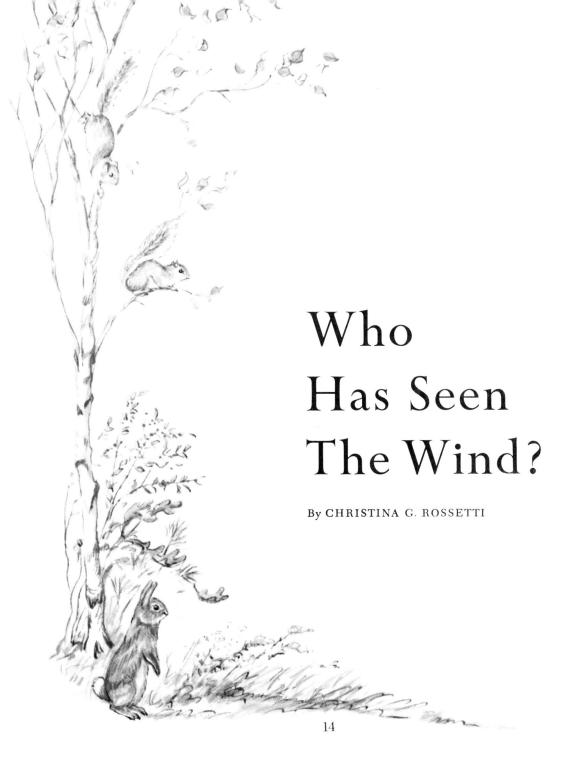

Who Has Seen The Wind?

By CHRISTINA G. ROSSETTI

Who has seen the wind?
    Neither I nor you:
But when the leaves hang trembling
    The wind is passing through.

Who has seen the wind?
    Neither you nor I:
But when the trees bow down their heads
    The wind is passing by.

At the Seaside

By ROBERT LOUIS STEVENSON

When I was down beside the sea
A wooden spade they gave to me
To dig the sandy shore.
My holes were empty like a cup,
In every hole the sea came up,
Till it could come no more.

Dairy Charm

Come, butter, come; come, butter, come.
  Peter stands at the gate
Waiting for his buttered cake;
  Come, butter, come.

Seventeenth Century

The Hayloft

By ROBERT LOUIS STEVENSON

Through all the pleasant meadow-side
    The grass grew shoulder-high,
Till the shining scythes went far and wide
    And cut it down to dry.

Those green and sweetly smelling crops
    They led in wagons home;
And they piled them here in mountain tops
    For mountaineers to roam.

Here is Mount Clear, Mount Rusty-Nail,
    Mount Eagle and Mount High;—
The mice that in these mountains dwell,
    No happier are than I!

Oh, what a joy to clamber there,
    Oh, what a place to play,
With the sweet, the dim, the dusty air,
    The happy hills of hay!

Over the River
and Through the Wood

By LYDIA MARIA CHILD

Over the river and through the wood,
   To grandfather's house we go;
      The horse knows the way
      To carry the sleigh
Through the white and drifted snow.

Over the river and through the wood—
   Oh, how the wind does blow!
      It stings the toes
      And bites the nose,
As over the ground we go.

Over the river and through the wood
   Trot fast, my dapple-gray!
     Spring over the ground,
     Like a hunting hound!
For this is Thanksgiving Day.

Over the river and through the wood,
   And straight to the barnyard gate.
     We seem to go
     Extremely slow,—
It is so hard to wait!

Over the river and through the wood,
   Now grandmother's cap I spy!
     Hurrah for the fun!
     Is the pudding done?
Hurrah for the pumpkin pie!

The Star

By JANE TAYLOR

Twinkle, twinkle, little star,
How I wonder what you are,
Up above the world so high,
Like a diamond in the sky.

When the blazing sun is set,
And the grass with dew is wet,
Then you show your little light,
Twinkle, twinkle, all the night.

Then the traveler in the dark
Thanks you for your tiny spark;
He could not see which way to go
If you did not twinkle so.

In the dark blue sky you keep,
And often through my curtains peep,
For you never shut your eye
Till the sun is in the sky.

As your bright and tiny spark
Lights the traveler in the dark,
Though I know not what you are,
Twinkle, twinkle, little star.

The
Rock-a-by Lady

By EUGENE FIELD

The Rock-a-by Lady from Hushaby Street
   Comes stealing; comes creeping;
The poppies they hang from her head to her feet,
And each hath a dream that is tiny and fleet—
She bringeth her poppies to you, my sweet,
   When she findeth you sleeping!

There is one little dream of a beautiful drum—
   "Rub-a-dub!" it goeth;
There is one little dream of a big sugarplum,
And lo! thick and fast the other dreams come
Of popguns that bang, and tin tops that hum
   And a trumpet that bloweth!

And dollies peep out of those wee little dreams
   With laughter and singing;
And boats go a-floating on silvery streams,
And the stars peek-a-boo with their own
     misty gleams,
And up, up, and up, where the Mother
     Moon beams,
The fairies go winging!

Would you dream all these dreams that are
    tiny and fleet?
   They'll come to you sleeping;
So shut the two eyes that are weary, my sweet,
For the Rock-a-by Lady from Hushaby Street,
With poppies that hang from her head to her feet,
   Comes stealing; comes creeping.

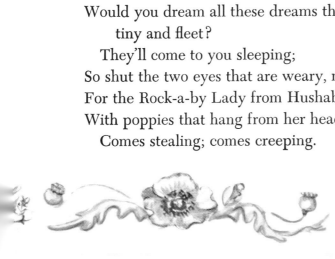

The Slumber Boat

By ALICE C. D. RILEY

Baby's boat's the silver moon,
Sailing in the sky,
Sailing o'er the sea of sleep,
While the clouds float by.

Sail, baby, sail,
Out upon that sea,
Only don't forget to sail,
Back again to me.

Baby's fishing for a dream,
　　Fishing near and far,
His line a silver moonbeam is,
　　His bait a silver star.

　　Sail, baby, sail,
　　　　Out upon that sea,
　　Only don't forget to sail,
　　　　Back again to me.

Wings

Oh that I had wings like a dove!
For then would I fly away and be at rest.
Lo, then would I wander far off,
And remain in the wilderness.

A Psalm of David

Born in Boston, Tasha Tudor grew up on a farm in Connecticut, and her impressions of rural New England life are the inspiration for her artwork. She has won many awards and honors since her first book was published in 1938. More than sixty books later, her gift is still unique. She now lives in Vermont where she is surrounded by her corgis, her family, and her friends—and the country pleasures so lovingly depicted in her books.